PEACH
PIG

PEACH PIG

CECILIA KNAPP

corsair ⟫ poetry

CORSAIR

First published in the United Kingdom in 2022 by Corsair

3 5 7 9 10 8 6 4 2

Epigraph from 'Lament', Mary Ruefle (*The Poetry Review*, 111.2), 2021

A CIP catalogue record for this book
is available from the British Library.

ISBN: 978-1-4721-5681-5

Printed and bound in Great Britain by
Clays Ltd, Elcograf S.p.A.

Papers used by Corsair are from well-managed forests
and other responsible sources.

Corsair
An imprint of
Little, Brown Book Group
Carmelite House
50 Victoria Embankment
London EC4Y 0DZ

An Hachette UK Company
www.hachette.co.uk

www.littlebrown.co.uk

How do I lament
it forth, this feeling of trying?
-MARY RUEFLE

Contents

PEACH
PIG

I Used to Eat KFC Zingers Without Hating Myself

Order cat litter off Amazon. Light a fig
candle. The clouds are a paper mouth.
Another Tesco Express. Someone else
has died on Facebook. The cat licks me.
Feel endorsed. Wonder if my therapist
thinks I'm a brat. Imagine her telling me
I'm her favourite. Get sad
that cancer got Alan Rickman.
Vit D spray under my tongue.
Himalayan salt rock.
Get drunk off my oat latte.
Man on the train slams into me.
Ask him to hold me
till I'm gorgeous.
Handle my cat's shit. Replay my own voice notes.
Speculate how carpet shops still make money.
Dream of dying. Watch
World's Strongest Man.
My father's angry prostate.
The men on the train could kill me.
I'm a pig. I need a pat on the back.
I need a thigh gap. I use emojis
to avoid conflict. Worry I'm a gentrifier.
Send that gif that everyone's seen before.

Someone I know has won an award.
I have a memory of your love
like a lodged fishbone.
Before you died, I cut your hair.

LOROS

I watched my mother form her new body.
Cheekbones becoming violent,
hips clucking to meet skin.
I would wash her as she used to wash me,
holding a small plastic jug
under the warm water
and tipping it over her back,
her edges broken by bubbles.

That night was like any other night
in the hospice, people quietly dying,
except we ate ham and pineapple pizza
in her bed. Watch out for the men, she said,
they have the upper hand. She smelt salty,
shoulders poured into a wipe-clean pillow.
The next day, when the doctor said she needed
to eat more, she laughed,
told him she had waited forever to be
this thin. I laughed with her.
When I try to replay her voice
I can't. This small slice is what I have.
A woman happy with her own shrinking
in the last weeks of her life.

My Mother Quit Bread

and yes, I let a man who sometimes loved me
flip me onto my stomach, pennies falling from his jeans.

I considered the sea,
salting my brother's eczema.

You're someone's son, I thought,
as the man went to town on me, how hilarious.

The picture of my mother people love most
is the one where she's wearing washing-up gloves.

I've lost count of the men.
My skin, a glowing pig.

Granddad used to kick Granny around the farm.
Men will calm down in the end, she said,

keep quiet. Bad husbands can become good
but dead women can only ever be dead.

When Dad left Mum, Mum cited
not enough bonking.

The woman he left her for wore
linen shirts. If a mother is absent,

her daughter becomes a scab
on an elbow, a wild, wet ruby.

The aunties in my family
tapped their teeth knowingly

before destroying a fresh pack
of ready salted crisps.

Daydream

Driving with my mother –
Scotland some days. The windows down, a strange heat.
Patsy Cline on the radio, so young my mother says,
plane crash, only thirty.
She was wearing a blue dress, a wristwatch found in the wreckage.
I'm grown. It's me driving, my wrist switching the gear.

On the Farm

What do I know about anything
except the feeling of watching the bull
make his muscular approach.
The heifers gently graze,
waiting for him, their large eyes focused
on the grass, till I open the gate,
get closer, fear rising. I unravel a light chain
from hollow bars.
They stop then, all look up at once,
as though they are a singular unit.
No sounds now
except a gunshot, pillowed by the woods,
the heavy tread of the bull across the hardened field
and my own heart beneath my fleece.
What a thrill to know he'll make his way
to each of them, mount them mechanically,
how they'll take it.

Portrait of My Brother as Cindy Crawford

Fishslick in gold lamé,
Grandma's clip-ons weighing down your lobes,
chopstick in your mouth like a cigarette,
God you could move, kid,
strutting down the landing,
your runway,
stopping, spinning by the VHS,
popping a peachy shoulder
to the blue leggings drying
on the banister,
thin hips, headlights.
You were luminous, warm-bodied.
You walked your eczema up
and down till you forgot
you were a boy.
You hadn't had
your lip bust up yet,
not in a house
of women, all eyes on you,
all our mum's scarves
around your throat.

Seascape

The mist hangs its low grey breasts,
a pitbull scoffs up pebbles.
The man in the shrimp shack sits like a joke,
how many women have run from their homes
to the sea?

*

How long will I be in the lung of this town?
All my clothes are stained.
A Fosters can hurls itself
into the water.

Some Older Dude

is outside Dad's house
chewing his cheeks
gargling a shadow
he can't come in
he has a car
dented boot
I lock the front door
behind me
my name hangs
from a pink keyring
he drives
roads and roads
till I don't recognise
the way home

at the petrol station
he buys a bottle
one cigarette
between us
Christmas swings
from the rear-view
I lean sideways
to kiss the blond
grit on his chin
my neck sliced
by the seatbelt

his scent quickens
Lynx rising
hot tongue
bleached mint
I'm all worship
a seal pup
legs newly slick
from my dad's razor

the next day
I trap Meg
in south block loos
orange foundation smearing
the sinks
I tell her
it still hurts
but it was good
no honestly it was good
walking home
a van honks
I yank my hem
to my knees
wave

Seascape

Schoolkids
fingers inside each other
Sub of the Day
a velcro wallet
staying up late
getting damp
in their cheap polos
chatting on pebbles
till the water is black

I was grotesque with summer, haloed

and freckled with light.
I gave up shoes for months,
read books on concrete steps.
I had a perfect little life, it was clear,
a rosy glow to my hands and face
even when asleep in a cold room.
Boys followed me politely round the quad
offering smooth cigarettes.
It was a different time!
I was thin as a racing dog, a flimsy thing
you could throw in the air
but I don't remember going hungry,
we didn't need food back then,
not in the same way.
I stayed up late most nights –
we all agreed that sleep was feeble.
My dead mum gave me a certain edge,
a useful note of sympathy.
I threw my look together with a flourish,
wore my grandma's clothes. A better time, simpler.
You could pick up an old car
for less than a hundred quid, and drive it
with no seatbelt,
right down the cost with men
you hardly knew.
Sure, a few of us had bruises

but boy did we know how to pump a clutch.
We were happy with our lot.
The world was pouring in on me, a barrel of ripe fruit
tipped over my head and I was sticky,
it was stunning.
My father had plenty of work, always seemed to be away.
People sent letters; it was a golden age!
There was that brief and sick bout of the weepies
that left me under the bridge in a tangle of blankets,
there was the sex on the floor of a basement
but it was still a misty joy to be alive.
And there was my brother
teetering, circling the drain,
but we were stronger then, didn't need as much,
kept smiling and saying it could be worse.
Besides, I was pretty good at scooping him back up.
We made a game of it, a frivolous time! Magic!
The whole damn seaside tinged in pink
like the sun could set forever.

Ain't You a Peach

I can be a show pony
when I want a cash tip.
I know they think of me
later in my tight jeans
whilst their quiet sons
eat baked potatoes.
I was a kid once.
I imagined a room
full of men in suits
ordering two fingers
of whiskey.
I touched myself
on a camp bed.
To get to the room
you have to drive
down a long motorway
in a smoke-filled car.
You have to know
about motorways.
I'm a basic girl;
strawberry chapstick,
cheap, flimsy dresses.
Sometimes I'm flattered
when they shout from vans.
My cousin once pinned me against the wall
with his mouth.

I had a hamster
and a CD player.
He arrived nervous
but his hands knew
how to slide a bolt.
I didn't give
but I stood still.
My auntie says
one day the whistles will stop
and I'll miss them.
He's married now, two boys.
Don't we all just want that,
a good night's sleep?

Daydream

I eat a whole loaf
of sliced white bread.

You Know a Market Where the Tulips Are Still Three Quid

and you buy them to remind yourself that you can.
They begin tight-lipped and upright,
but their petals become loose, droop.
Their stems start to lean away from their own.
You know the cat will cry at two a.m.,
some nights you will sleep right through,
others your body will fling you upright as though
your brother is dying. You know what the wine does
to your teeth. You know about leaving.
You know how to keep useless things
in case you need to build a shrine.
You know how to make gods of men
whose toothbrushes sit caked on the kitchen counter.
You know and you let them weigh your avocado,
rolling it around in their palm.

All My Ex-Boyfriends Are Having a Dinner Party

comparing their tight obliques,
how red their meat, hat tricks
for their grassroots teams,
wearing expensive suits,
saying they had me in a car once,
I never kept my mouth shut,
I always wanted to stay the night.
I'm dieting again, sipping low-cal miso
on a moving train, burning my hands.
I smile at other joggers, I'm enjoying this.
The dentist says I have yellow teeth,
his hands hold my tongue.
Mum said you can do anything
as long as you're wearing
washing-up gloves.

A purple leaflet in the waiting room
asks me if life has worked out
a) better
b) worse
c) the same
For one thousand pounds
I can fix my teeth.
Mum used to ballroom dance

a wooden spoon, weeping with the radio.
I've been keeping my fallen eyelashes in a bag,
I spit pink foam into the sink, decide
this week I'll only eat eggs
till the days smudge.
I see people eating crisps in public
on a Monday
like they have no guilt.

The Leaves Dreamy Green

I want my mum to make me corned beef hash.
I've been justifying long sleeps: essential cell repair.
I've been French knitting. I've regressed.
Somewhere a man is telling a woman to take off her clothes.
How did we get here?
OK, there's a beautiful forest
but I'm nowhere near it.
He uses the term 'fuller figure'.
Some questions:
If a man swings his dick in the wood…
How many times have I wished I could've put my clothes back on?
Here goes the dance where I reach for the light switch.
I used to sleep for hours after he left.
Sometimes he would ask me to clean his room.
And when I finally woke,
that's the first thing I did.

Tuesday

I stare at the carpet
till it's time to turn the telly on.
I try to find that picture of you
swimming in green water, shaking
the fin of a dolphin.

I consider the salt content of soy sauce,
then throw my lunch
down the stairs, weep
at the way daylight
haloes a lettuce leaf.

I yell at the flat,
grab a fistful of belly on the toilet.

Charlie sends me a photo of her lunch.
Figs, Parma ham. <3
Another friend of mine
is a mother twice over. I can't even drive.

In the supplement,
Jenny the exec, from Highbury,
is up at four-thirty a.m.,
packs the kids' lunches, tennis
then smoothie.

I'm staring at the carpet.

I Google female scuba stars
who've touched the deepest parts of the ocean,

tuck myself into the TV
to binge on murdered women.

Television

The truth teller with an oxygen tube in his nose
is the first one shot on a murky island. The hiss
of his tank turned off. Another cover up, another
sad dad in a limp anorak with a picture of his missing girl.
There is always a boy found in the woods, his distant mother
advancing the plot. There's always two wine glasses by the sink.
And the news, of course, of your own approaching misery,
a pasture waiting. Very soon from now, your body will bulge
like a bag of rats, your clothes, drab over the strain
of your belly, stretched and lately overlooked.
You thought you were different. You had dreams.
You were attentive to the possibility of your own unhappiness,
which rendered you immune. Sorry but no, kid.
                    This is what it looks like:
from the vantage point of your Ford Focus, you see the blurred outline
of the man you love through the curtains, the man you gave
things up for. Greyer, granted, less lean, but seasoned and keen
with the rush of blood to his cock. You'll see him pull off the top
of the younger neighbour with the small breasts that indicate intelligence.
The English rain will meet you there. Your life, churning out its credits.

Daydream

I execute an arm balance in my yoga class.
The teacher is impressed, I can tell.
During relaxation I picture nothing
but ripples on water. I am strong
in body, in mind. I meditate
without thinking of dinner.

Your Membership Arrives
in a Peach Envelope

Keep yourself empty, nothing more
than the size of a man's fist inside you.
Breakfast is snow.
Lunch, a smooth boiled egg, cooled to room temperature.
At first, you are glorious. Gross with beauty,
buffed up like a bleached teaspoon.
There's an app with a subscription and pastel graphics
to log your weekly failures. There are gifts.
A sea salt candle. A cloth doll to house your doubts.
There are oaths. Push notifications.
If you sink a pill in yoghurt it's like you never took it.
You start to hover, spectral, gliding,
serene for your latte.
You are spun sugar, when the sun catches you right.
Even your pussy is a tight pink lettuce.
Are you sick of the sight of yourself?
Something in your path?
Blink again.
Your neck gets longer, you are ascending.
I'm a bloody marvel, you think,
before you notice the puddle on the doormat,
start to bump into things, leaking
salty weather all over the bathroom.
Are you currently present?

Are you choosing the path of a victim?
You stare at fast trains to keep you grounded.
You can't remember when the tiredness started.
At night you hear a tide slapping against a cave.
Your limbs are all breath, a lilo turned over in the wind.
Your fingertips fog.
You find that people only have to put a gentle hand on your head
and you open your mouth right up.
By now, you're fully lost in the soup of it.
Keep going, girl.
This means it's working.
Now you can bend over in the light.
Now you tell him, thank you.
Now you are small enough
to sit on his knee.

yoga

today she says
we are opening our hips
the purple room
the eucalyptus

the first time
you sucked bathwater
into yourself

what about the boy
in your sleeping bag?
your eyes clamped shut

there's a hole
in the ground
in the woods
by your grandma's house

waiting on the street
in shorts (the first warm day)
neon trainers
a man approaches you
do you run?
he says

and the sky is so blue
he could be harmless

this might hurt
she says
when we open our hips
our purple rooms
you might cry after
we hold a lot of memory
there; the hinge
of our flexors
the hiss
of our breath

ever seen
inside yourself
with a camera?
pink and viscous
the conch in mum's
old downstairs loo
you watch on the monitor
like it's not even your body
as you open and receive
the probe

later, you bookmark
a difficult page
with your colposcopy results
your cervix is technically fine
it's emotional
your bleeding
nothing *bodily*

in bed, he touches you
and you feel a stiff fish
in the belly
of a rowing boat

you think of all the times
you've been touched
and held your face
in a neutral expression
breathing through hello

you're supposed to want it
what's your lack?
all that promise
untapped power

there was a time
when you weren't real
without a hand on you
you could get hot
for brutal men

the man who left you
face down on the bed
when you were nineteen
doesn't think of it now
he's in a conservatory
with his wife
on his mobile phone
digesting a piece of bread

Spritz

OK, you're a guilty pig,
but walk down Broadway Market
with a £9 drink in a plastic cup.
Forget your dad working raw,
the insides of hospitals, it's fine,
you're one of these people now.
Just drift down the market, you deserve
the air-pockety bread.
Admit it, you're taken in,
you are impossible
with delight, with the scent
of coffee bean. You admire
floor-to-ceiling windows, gaze
at the drowsy girl
in high-waisted trousers,
a rust shirt, slim wrists.
Give up trying to hate it,
you're a rotten peach,
aren't you,
clinging to its stone.
This isn't about how
you couldn't afford to save
your brother's life,
Dad's roll-out bed.
Brush the crumbs from your cashmere
girl, what's the point of feeling bad

all the time? Get soaked with it,
have the salted butter, the altar.
You are present,
return to the breath,
to the podcast.
You will birth babies
so quick you'll shock the midwife.
You can be tight as a drum
with the right classes,
a privately-educated husband
who will grill meat.
You can have the small violet cakes,
the quiet terror
of the high-rise looming
at the bottom of your garden.

The bees are on the roof

in their custom-made hives.
A new coffee machine
the size of a small head.
Rubbish smoulders on the lawns.
The smoke comes blowsy
and smelling
of burnt hair.
Chaos, sure,
but we're not running yet.
Men still get angry
when they're hungry.
Or when you've pushed them.
If you dress it all up
in a bad wig, the rot
don't stink.
What can I tell you?
I'm a sucker for it all.
A glutinous daughter.
Nodding my head like
isn't it terrible?
Imagine I'm God for once:
bless my pillowy self,
all its baggy lack.
Night falls in navy curtains.
Oh, to sleep,
to sleep like a man.

Daydream

My brother comes over for dinner.
He knocks on the door and I answer.
He's got a bottle of red in one hand, the man he loves in the other.
Come in, I say, I've made spag bol, like Mum did.
My hair is a messy up-do, I look radiant, effortless
with an apron on. My brother has quit drinking
and shoves me the bottle.
My brother has let himself love a man.
We eat. We talk through the night.

your head in the window

meant you weren't out
trying to score

you said you weren't high
it was the pebbles

on the drive
made you walk funny

you're a wreck, lad
you'll end up

down the farmyard
rolling with the pigs

it wasn't you
when the money went missing

we did normal things too, hot milk,
fags in the woods, you on look-out

I still dream you
in the green birches, shivering

tender, boy, you did all the things
brothers were good for

someone can love you
and still break your nose, you told me,

after you did
and I forgave you

right there on the bus
with all the blood

Bust-up Lip

Come in from the cold, babe,
your glasses are all smashed up.
You say it don't hurt,
don't wanna be touched,
cleaned up, but it's raining,
hard, green Brighton rain.
You disappear up your tree
with your hands on fire
in the new tracksuit
you saved up for,
you're invisible
against the night, hiding
the long limbs
you were born into.
You don't want to play footy,
you want to dance purple,
feel the slick untwist of a lippy.
You want the girls from the estate,
who let you kiss them exactly
because you don't like it.
They show you how drink works,
they are goddesses,
blue eyeshadow,
smart mouths,
I love them,
they always bring you home.

Seascape

My brother talks
knee-deep with the sea.
I pull him out,
we twitch like fish.

How many times
has it taken a body
beneath its softness?

My Brother Quit Drinking Maybe Five Times

and yes, those days were just about keeping him alive,
waiting for sleep, the water running backwards,
cutting grapes in two, arranging them on stairs,
filling him up with mash on Fridays.
But this isn't about that. It's not about how the sunlight
was too complicated, how he watched yellow cartoons in the dark,
eating rice in a soft cape.
It's not about how his hands were the most dangerous thing he owned.
Let it be instead about community radio, the soft pouch
of a volunteer's belly, the smell of soap,
and his voice.
Let this one be about taking his glasses off
when he fell asleep on the sofa.
It's not about the time it went nasty purple, his hand
crashing into my father's head. This one's about eating sausages, and a new bike,
a story recorded on a cassette tape. Christ, this one's about
the tracksuit he saved up for, not the hospital again, it's not about
the foaming plastic bottles, how the world made him hate the taste
of himself. It's not another poem about a boy, or the sea,
or how I pulled a knife from his hand, his eyes small darknesses.
I'm thinking about how he loved trains and dresses,
and the man with the gold hair at his funeral
who took my wrists in both his hands and said to me,
I promise, we had a good thing.

on good days my brother

is smiling
there's no bottle
no thick night phone call
as he looks down
at a city
from a balcony
thinking about flying
a hot spoon
in his hand
the shadows
he left on the stairs
have gone
like smoke
he is dancing
into the widest summer
in a long red dress

I'm Shouting, I LOVED YOUR DAD at My Brother's Cat

I'm crying at green wallpaper
sick with the memory of your hands.
When you died, though I'd asked you not to,
I got some rest. Fair play. I ate my eggs, and the sun came out.
How do you enjoy a fuck when you're sunburnt with grief.
I had hoped for a loss of appetite, some silver lining.
I live in a flat that I can't afford. It's got big windows.
They get so dirty. I don't condition my hair.
You'd be disappointed at how often I let myself go.
I've got your name tattooed on my finger, but it keeps falling off
when I do the washing up.
I've kept that cat you poured your tenderness into.
I don't remember kissing you
but that doesn't mean it didn't happen.
Some days it's someone else's brother.
You serve me in a coffee shop, you're on the mend,
pierced ears and a soft hat.

Designated Survivor

On daytime TV, a pleasant interview
that skims lightly.

The crisis we are all talking about,
explained. The stink of myself.

Two peaches rot in the bowl, the yielding
fuzz of them like unfused skulls.

Orphaned rat babies in the labs want the soft cloth
mother, even though the wire dummy has the milk.

It gets to you eventually. Being the one to live on,
my body an imperfect seal for all my liquids.

At night I imagine the sound of drones
tracking across the sky,

the hopeful sardine fishermen
out there in dark water.

The kids are hungry, throwing
tennis balls against the new build.

A current moves the curtain
almost imperceptibly.

Count on my fingers how much I can take,
prod the comfortable mass of his body, digesting,

picture the pulp of a tumour blooming
in his soft stomach. So what? The world

is smouldering. Night unhooks itself.
The things we are capable of doing to each other.

Sometimes when I close my eyes, the outline of a boy arrives
like I've been staring at a bright light.

I LOVE YOU, ECHO

the little lad shouts
as he passes
under the bridge
his voice returns to him
on he goes with
his blue scooter
ants fly thick as sex
what certainty do I have
here cramping and sweating
while my cat sheds
another month
blood in the toilet blooming
dark peony
I hope that boy has
a soft father
who sings him
to sleep

I Hope You Stopped for the Swans

It's hard to recognise longing
filling up the body like a rock pool.
Looking behind me at the wall.
Why is it always four o'clock?

I hear knocking when I'm sleeping,
but don't see your face anymore.
Come inside. Shake the water off, my love,
you've had a skinful.

Somewhere our dad is on a hill
with his waterproof map.
He'll send me a long text later about
being at London Bridge, eating a Cornish pasty.

I'll reply, 'Renationalise the railways!'
by which I mean, I love you
and I'm sorry your son died.
How we used to beg him to bury us in the sand.

There are small mercies; my soft father.
I don't think about him crumbling apart
on the kitchen stool,
how seven minutes later he was back to normal,

singing under his breath, spreading apricot jam.
The sky is thin today
like a torn-off blister
and he is underneath it, walking.

Seascape

I put my ear to the sea.
Ring, ring.
The sea answers,
Hello, you small idiot.
Just for the fun of it I ask
if I could drink my brother's ashes back.

Everywhere Else Is Always Better

You want dark sand,
a road lined with redwoods,
to swim in a river
without your body chasing you.
You want the smoke before the cancer,
soft American light,
the beaded doors and the heat,
a small tray of meat for lunch.
Why do cowboy films comfort old men?
Strap on some good boots
and walk the world, big dog!
Sleep without the guilt,
the terrible green dreams.
Oh to drive down a farm road
wearing a hat. Eat a cherry
in a light breeze, listening
to the type of music
only heard through windows.
Watch a grandfather cry softly
on a plastic chair, moved by a violin.
You want to be exhausted
from growing vegetables,
leaning against an upright fork,
a scarecrow waving from the next field.

Sometimes a doctor marvels

at the size of a tumour, privately,
with a friend, raking the crisps
from the pub table with his hand after
a long shift. Like, woah. She was a beauty.

A small boy slips on his sister's mermaid dress
and his body feels right beneath the purple gauze.

Farmers get lonely, rolling over the clods of dirt
in a violet morning, where the seat of their tractor
is worn to the metal.

Sometimes the thing happens just like in a film.
The girl dabs the blood from the brother's brow
in the school toilets with a wet tissue.

There's nothing you can do to stop the wind,
the hiss of the cig tip hitting the water.

Acknowledgements

I would like to thank the editors of the following magazines where some of these poems were published in their baby stages: *Magma*, *bath magg*, *Perverse*, *Ambit*, *Wasafiri*, *Popshot*, *Granta* and *The White Review*. Thank you also to *Bad Betty Press* for anthologising some of my early work.

Thank you, Polarbear A.K.A. Steven Camden for opening the heavy door of poetry, showing me what it could be and how to find it myself. Thank you to the Roundhouse and those who work there, past and present, for the opportunities you afford young writers.

Jess, Jack, Izzy, Maria, I am so lucky to have met you. Not only did we write together for that first bleary year, we became friends for life. Thank you for your encouragement when my poems were, frankly, awful.

Thank you to Apples and Snakes, Spread the Word, the Poetry Society, the Royal Society of Literature, Toast Poetry, Arvon, The Arts Council and everyone who works tirelessly within these organisations (and many others!) to support writers. You enable so many people who wouldn't have otherwise found their way here.

Wayne Holloway-Smith, you helped me transform my work. A heartfelt thank you for the rigour and enthusiasm with which you approached my poems and for your many insights.

Thank you Rachel Long, the most gifted, generous, fun, editor I know. Remember Hampstead Heath with the midges and the torch light and the pink wine? I won't forget it. You gave me the confidence to take my time, to trust myself. This book wouldn't exist without you. I am so lucky to call you my friend.

Thanks must also go to Jack Underwood, Shazea Quraishi, Caroline Bird, Mimi Khalvati, Arji Manuelpillai, Gboyega Odubanjo, Anthony Anaxagorou, Jess Murrain, Toby Campion, Alice Frecknall, Bridget Minamore, Bryony Littlefair, Elisabeth Sennitt Clough, Jemima Foxtrot, Talia Randall, Shruti Chauhan, Scroobius Pip, Martha Sprackland and every single person who has been kind enough to look at my work over all these years. I have met some amazing writers in my life. Some are my good friends now. There are too many list but I thank you for your warmth, time and grace.

To the people who have supported me by inviting me to read at gigs, write commissions, teach and participate in projects; thank you.

Thank you Becky, you are just so good.

Thank you Sarah Castleton who believed in these poems. Thank you to the whole team at Corsair; Phoebe, Hayley and everyone who works so hard to make books happen. Writing this book saved me many times over. To know it has found a place in the world means more than I can say.

Thank you to my family.

Thank you Luis for your patience and love and for the happiest home I have ever known.

Thank you to my friends. This book is for and because of you.

About the author

Cecilia Knapp is a poet and novelist and the Young People's Laureate for London 2020/2021. She was shortlisted for the 2022 Forward prize for best single poem. She is the winner of the 2021 Ruth Rendell award and has been shortlisted for both the Rebecca Swift Women's prize and the Outspoken poetry prize. Her poems have appeared in *The White Review*, *Granta*, *Wasafiri*, *Popshot*, *Ambit*, *Magma* and *bath magg*. She curated the anthology *Everything is Going to be All Right: Poems for When you Really Need Them*, published by Trapeze in 2021. Her debut novel *Little Boxes* is published by The Borough Press. She teaches poetry and creative writing in a number of settings and lives in London.

A list of organisations offering support

Women's Aid
www.womensaid.org.uk

National Domestic Abuse Helpline
www.nationalhelpline.org.uk
0808 2000 247

CALM
www.thecalmzone.net
0800 585858

Samaritans (24/7 service)
116 123

Mind
www.mind.org.uk

BEAT
www.beateatingdisorders.org.uk

Turning Point
www.turning-point.co.uk

Action addiction
www.actionaddiction.org.uk
020 3981 5525

Support for family members of alcoholics
www.al-anonuk.org.uk
www.alcoholchange.org.uk

The Mix, free information and support for under 25s in the UK
www.themix.org.uk
0808 808 4994

National LGBT+ Domestic Abuse Helpline
www.galop.org.uk
0800 999 5428

Coping with bereavement
www.familylives.org.uk